Elder Abuse:
Approaches to Working with Violence

Bridget Penhale and Jonathan Parker
with Paul Kingston

VENTURE PRESS

© Bridget Penhale and Jonathan Parker
with Paul Kingston, 2000

BASW website: http://www.basw.co.uk

Published by
VENTURE PRESS
16 Kent Street
Birmingham
B5 6RD

British Library Cataloguing-in-Publication Data
A catalogue record for this book is available from the
British Library

ISBN 1 86178 047 8   (paperback)

Cover design by:
Western Arts
194 Goswell Road
London
EC1V 7DT

Printed in Great Britain by Hobbs the Printers Ltd.

Contents

Dedication

For our families, colleagues and, most of all our parents.

Introduction: Protection and the context of elder abuse

We all have some idea of what it means to protect. It may be that the immediate image that comes to mind is one of a vulnerable person, a child perhaps, who is in some kind of danger of harm or injury. The term carries with it a sense that the protector has the right, responsibility or power to protect and that the protected individual is in need of this protection. In this way the concept of protection contributes to our understanding of the rules according to which society operates and individuals interact with one another. It is also important to understanding how social and health care practitioners operate. This volume concerns the protection of vulnerable older people and the response to this by social and health care professionals.

In social work, protection is popularly associated with children and families. However it also refers to the protection of adults who are vulnerable because of a mental health problem, a physical disability or a learning disability. Of course, this includes older people. Individuals may be vulnerable in two ways: because of the actions of other people towards them or because their own actions or neglect of themselves put themselves at some degree of risk (Figure 1.1).

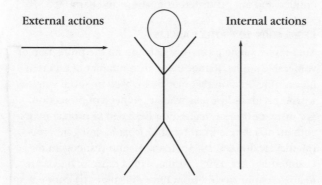

Figure 1.1 Directions of vulnerability

When seeking to protect people, social workers practice in ways that are both caring and controlling. By this we mean that social workers work to provide services and assistance to the individuals that allow them to make decisions in a safe and enabling way and to continue the lifestyle of their choice. Conversely it may refer to the controlling actions that regulate and sometimes prevent individuals from living in the way they choose (Figure 1.2).

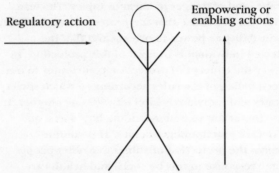

Regulatory action

Empowering or enabling actions

Figure 1.2 Protective actions

Care and control are essential elements of the social work task. One may enter a career in the helping professions because of a deep-rooted commitment to the care of vulnerable, disadvantaged and excluded people. This may require a protective role for the practitioner in working to prevent exploitation at the individual, group or social level. Such a commitment can also imply a degree of control in using the laws of the state to ensure that people are granted their rights, receive the care to which they are entitled and are protected from abuse and harm.

LEGISLATION TO PROTECT ADULTS

There is no single piece of legislation on the protection of vulnerable adults. Rather there are a number of different pieces of legislation that may be invoked by social workers working with individuals who are in need of protection. For instance there is legislation designed to protect people with mental illness from harm or from harming others (Mental Health Act, 1983; Mental Health (Patients in the Community) Act, 1995). Adults with a range of needs are to an extent protected from life's difficulties by entitlement to an assessment and services to meet identified needs

(National Health Service and Community Care Act, 1990). The Sexual Offences Act, 1957 offers protection against unwanted sexual advances; the Protection from Harassment Act, 1997 offers protection against bullying and stalking. The Family Law Act, 1996 (Part IV) offers some protection against violence in the domestic setting. The social worker may, as we shall consider when discussing interventions, use these aspects of legislation to regulate and control or to empower and enable vulnerable older adults. The aim of protection in social and health care involves both aspects.

PREVENTIVE WORK

Prevention is much talked about in social work and allied professions as a way of working with people considered to be in need of protection. Browne and Herbert (1997) identify three levels of prevention:

- Primary
- Secondary
- Tertiary

Primary prevention refers to policy and actions taken before a situation becomes a problem. It accounts for any needs before the potential for harm and danger becomes apparent. As social workers and health care professionals, it is imperative that we keep up to date with policy changes and new legislation. By contributing to consultation papers on new policy initiatives and by acting through professional bodies such as the British Association of Social Workers or The Royal College of Nurses, we are able to bring experience and knowledge from practice to bear on its development.

Secondary prevention relates to people who are identified as in potential need of protection before the point where an abusive act or situation arises. Assessment under the National Health Service and Community Care Act, 1990 allows social care practitioners to assess the needs of individuals and to develop a plan of care with the service users to meet those needs.

Tertiary protection refers to intervention and services after an actual protection issue has been identified, for instance when an act of physical violence or emotional abuse has already occurred. The objective of acting at this stage is to reduce or minimise the risk of harm reoccurring in the future. This may require immediate and authoritative action. The Mental Health Act, 1983 or respite care services might be employed here, for example. It is at this stage that a number of ethical dilemmas can occur for practitioners. It is often the case that measures taken at this level are *imposed* on the persons experiencing the abuse, thus potentially abusing them again but in the name of protection. This demonstrates the need to consolidate legal measures governing social work responses to the abuse of older people and vulnerable adults in general. What it demands of practitioners is to ask such questions as *Who is the client?*, *What are the client's wishes?*, *What is the least restrictive course of action?*, and then acting.

THE ROLE OF THE SOCIAL AND HEALTH CARE PROFESSIONAL IN DOMESTIC VIOLENCE

We need to consider the role of social and health care workers in the broader context of domestic violence before looking in particular at elder abuse. In doing so, we are not suggesting that elder abuse is simply one point along a continuum of domestic violence. The definitional complexities involved in considering elder abuse preclude such a simplistic approach. Elder abuse covers a much broader spectrum than abuse in domestic settings alone, as we shall see later.

There are important lessons to be learned from some of the mistakes and failures of social workers working in the area of domestic violence. According to a number of authors and reports, social and health care workers have contributed to the minimisation of the problem of domestic violence (Department of Health/Social Services Inspectorate, 1996; Mullender, 1996). They have ignored referrals that suggest the existence of violence and abuse and demonstrated a great lack of knowledge. However, health and social care workers are now making more referrals to Women's Aid and other voluntary organisations, and are more valued for the practical help and assistance they provide. A similar situation has existed concerning the involvement of health and social care workers in relation to elder abuse.

Social and health care workers still have considerable ground to make up in relation to the development of their role in situations of domestic violence generally (in the broadest sense of the term). The role of the health and social care worker should be broad and wide-ranging. It may include:

- Making immediate practical arrangements to ensure safety.
- Identifying the legal position and the availability of social supports, taking cultural factors into account.
- Assessing the risk to the individual and any other vulnerable parties in the relationship.
- Providing advice, support and information.
- Contributing to public and professional awareness-raising and education.
- Working individually to deal with the effects of violence and abuse.
- Working with families to maintain safety.
- Working with abusers to control anger and to develop strategies to prevent abuse from occurring or reoccurring.

This wide range of roles and tasks is located within the context of the laws governing social and health care responses, for instance eligibility for a community care assessment, support for a carer, assessment for compulsory admission to hospital under the Mental Health Act and so on. Also, the roles are protective in seeking to influence policy development at the local and national level, to provide a care and safety plan when risk is identified and to intervene after abuse has occurred, working with both abuser and abused. The roles and tasks are underpinned by social work and health care values that emphasise respect for individuals, privacy, choice and the maximisation of social and individual functioning.

A contemporary overview of elder abuse

It was not until the late 1970s that the first reports of elder abuse in domestic settings were published in the UK. These were written from the perspective of medical practice. However, only limited attention was given to the issue at that point, and it took until the late 1980s for there to be any real focus on the matter. Much of the work in the late 1980s and early 1990s was by professionals with a background in social work. Mervyn Eastman and Jacki Pritchard in particular have worked hard since that time to try to raise awareness of elder abuse and to develop professional responses to the problem. Attention to the problem by the government has, however, been much slower.

More recently, since the mid 1990s, elder abuse has been regarded in the UK as a discrete form of mistreatment, based on research mainly undertaken in North America. In 1993 the Social Services Inspectorate/Department of Health published the first document to acknowledge elder abuse as an issue of serious official concern, needing attention from welfare agencies (Social Services Inspectorate, 1993). Before then a variety of professionals and pressure groups had been raising awareness to try to obtain a response from the government. This was complemented by the development of adult protection/vulnerable adult policies, procedures and guidelines by some local authorities. A spate of guidelines was issued throughout the early 1990s. These were underpinned by a value base consistent with social work and social care, and promoted choice, privacy, independence, quality of life and safety (ibid.) Guidance on the development and implementation of policies and procedures has been issued to health and social care agencies involved in delivering care to older people (Department of Health, 2000). Local authority social services departments have the lead role in coordinating responses at the local level. The guidance document has Section 7 status, which means that the authorities at whom it is aimed *must* implement it. It is important to note that the response has been positioned within the context of social care values as opposed to the development of protective legislation and rights.

DEFINITIONS

Definition remains one of the most contentious areas in the debate on elder abuse. Bennett *et al.*, (1997) have noted a number of changes in the terms used over the years. These emphasise popular associations with gendered stereotypes that add little to social workers' understanding of wide-ranging abuse of older people in different settings. An example here is 'granny bashing', a term in used in the earliest days of recognition of the problem.

The most commonly used term in the UK is now 'elder abuse'. Whilst the actual definition of elder abuse remains disputed, there is some degree of agreement on the types of abuse covered by many of the recent definitions, as shown by the following quotation:

Abuse may be described as physical, sexual, psychological or financial. It may be intentional or unintentional or the result of neglect. It causes harm to the older person, either temporarily or over a period of time (Social Services Inspectorate, 1993).

The most recent definition is, however, much broader: 'Abuse is a violation of an individual's human and civil rights by any other person or persons' (Department of Health, 2000, 2.5).

Commentators generally describe the types of abuse as physical, psychological, material, sexual and neglect (see Box 1.1). Self-neglect is often omitted from the debate in the UK, but this form of neglect is easily the most prevalent in North America and demands the most resources from the adult protective services (APSs) – specialist teams created to deal with issues of abuse and protection in the United States. UK practitioners also deal with cases of self-neglect but without treating it as a category of abuse or neglect.

Box 1.1 CATEGORIES OF ABUSE

Physical abuse – causing physical harm, injury, physical coercion, sexual molestation and physical restraint.

Psychological abuse – causing mental anguish or emotional distress.

Material abuse – illegal or improper exploitation and/or use of funds or materials.

Active neglect – refusal or failure to undertake a care-giving obligation (including a conscious and intentional attempt to inflict physical harm or emotional stress on the elder).

Passive neglect – refusal or failure to fulfil a caring obligation (excluding a conscious and intentional attempt to inflict physical harm or emotional stress on the elder).

The UK national charity Action on Elder Abuse has developed a more extensive definition that implies a relationship between abuser and abused by including the term 'expectation of trust':

Elder abuse is a single or repeated act, or lack of appropriate action occurring within any relationship where there is an expectation of trust, which causes harm or distress to an older person (Action on Elder Abuse, 1995).

Bennett *et al.* (1997) have developed a taxonomy of abuse that considers the type of relationship between what has been crudely called 'victim' and 'perpetrator', alongside an analysis of the factors influencing abusive behaviours at the micro (individual), mezzo (community) and macro (political) levels of social relationships. A valid categorisation of elder abuse for social and health care practitioners can be drawn from this that acknowledges the interplay between structural, environmental and individual factors:

- *Social abuse* – ageist attitudes prevalent in society.
- *Political abuse* – the failure of the government and policy makers to provide legislation and encourage political will for change.
- *Community level abuse* – the development and maintenance of cultures that privilege one group above another. ►

- *Organisational abuse* – the failure of helping agencies and organisations to provide sufficient resources to deal with abuse.
- *Institutional abuse* – individual institutions fail to provide adequate care for individuals or actively promote an abusive regime.
- *Familial and domestic abuse* – individually directed abusive actions.

Elder abuse is a contentious topic upon which agreement has not yet been fully reached. Initially the focus of research was on abuse in domestic settings. However this has now widened. The types of abuse occurring and the levels at which abuse occurs in society are acknowledged and it is recognised that elder abuse also takes place in institutional settings. This is seen to be an enduring problem. The types of abuse that occur in institutional settings include the following:

- Lack of basic standards.
- Poor physical care and quality of life.
- The erosion of individuality.
- Resistance to change in geriatric care.
- Poor physical working conditions.
- Staff burn-out.
- Other organisational factors leading to inadequate standards of care.
- Fraud (including prescription fraud).
- Various types of restraint and prevention of risk-taking by residents.
- Murder.

This is not an exhaustive list. New forms of abuse are now being recognised, including forms of sensory deprivation (or overload), inadequate dietary provision and lack of care in the terminal stages of illness. Other forms of abuse may be related to 'lifestyle orientation', as the following quote illustrates:

Older lesbians argued, for instance, that those responsible for older people's homes should recognise the need for single sex homes and take into account the realities of lesbian family life (Curtis, 1993).

Elder abuse in institutional settings can also include mistreatment by families or other residents. It is not unknown for family members to attempt to obtain a signature in order to modify a will or misappropriate property or possessions. There are also situations where tensions between residents can cause both psychological and physical abuse to develop. Service providers clearly have a duty to protect their service users from abuse by other individuals. This includes family members, friends and acquaintances, other service users and members of staff. The value bases underpinning social and health care professionals in institutional settings demand the promotion of respect for individuals and their need for privacy, choice and protection. It is essential that social and health care professionals hold on firmly to these values in protecting those at risk of abuse in these situations.

INCIDENCE AND PREVALENCE OF ELDER ABUSE

There are two distinct ways of measuring the scale of social issues: prevalence and incidence. When considering elder abuse, the 'prevalence rate' refers to the number of older people in a specified population at any one time who share a certain characteristic (in this case, those who have been abused). The 'incidence rate', on the other hand, refers to the number of new cases of abuse occurring within a particular population (older people) over a specified period of time.

Generally, it is difficult to quantify elder abuse that takes place within the almost private realm of the family. Asking questions about intimate details of family interactions is fraught with difficulties. It is therefore not surprising that prevalence studies are limited. A nine-year prevalence figure of 1.6 per cent in the United States has been calculated from the longitudinal study by Lachs *et al*. (1997). From a UK perspective, the study by Ogg and Bennett (1991) has generated a degree of political agreement that elder abuse and neglect exist as a social problem. Their findings suggest that approximately 5 per cent of older people experience psychological abuse and 2 per cent physical or financial abuse.

An important incidence study was published in 1998 by the National Center on Elder Abuse at the American Public

Human Services Association (http://www.aoa.gov/abuse/report/Cexecsum.html), which method aimed to quantify the number of new cases of elder abuse within one year. Two sets of data were collected: statistics from APSs, and reports from 'sentinels'(individuals in frequent contact with elderly community residents). The study used definitions similar to the types of abuse listed above. The study highlighted that :

- Female elders are abused at a higher rate than males, even after accounting for their larger proportion in the ageing population.
- Older people aged 80 years and over are abused and neglected at two to three times the rate of their proportion in the elderly population.
- In almost 90 per cent of elder abuse and neglect incidents with a known perpetrator, the perpetrator is a family member, and two-thirds of perpetrators are adult children or spouses.
- Victims of self-neglect are usually depressed, confused or extremely frail.

The executive summary of the research suggests that approximately 450,000 elderly persons in domestic settings in the United States were abused and/or neglected during 1996. When older people who experienced self-neglect are added, the number increases to approximately 551,000. These figures can be crudely translated into an annual incidence of 1.12 per cent new cases. Perhaps the most significant statements relate to the percentage of relevant reports by the APSs or the sentinels:

The best national estimate is that a total of 449,924 elderly persons, aged 60 and over, experienced abuse and/or neglect in domestic settings in 1996. Of this total 70,942 (16 per cent) were reported to and substantiated by the APS agencies, but the remaining 378,982 (84 per cent) were not reported to APS agencies. One can conclude from these figures that over five times as many new incidents of elder abuse and neglect were unreported than those that were reported to and substantiated by APS agencies in 1996 (National Center on Elder Abuse, 1998, p 2, Executive summary).

Certainly, these prevalence and incidence figures suggest there is little doubt that elder abuse and neglect is a significant problem. However, whether welfare agencies actually receive reports of abuse is clearly an issue in view of the above data. What is lacking in the UK is a minimum data set that will collate standardised data from agencies (especially the lead agency – local authority social services departments). This would measure the magnitude of reports and substantiated cases. Perhaps social and health care practitioners skilled at asking difficult questions about intimate and private details of family life can assist in collecting this information.

RISK FACTORS

Research to date has produced limited insights into the risk factors that pertain to elder abuse and neglect. The main reason for this is the tendency to aggregate all forms of abuse together – this means that it has not been possible to identify distinct risk factors for differing forms or types of abuse. Whilst acknowledging the limitations of their study, Lachs *et al.* (1997, p 474) reiterate this point:

The outcome in this study included abuse, neglect and exploitation; it is conceivable that risk factors might be different for each and that our study is measuring an 'average' effect.

This is important to bear in mind given the increased and necessary emphasis on risk assessment in social and health care practice (Parsloe, 1999).

A series of case control studies reviewed by Bennett *et al.* (1997) are of relevance to a consideration of risk factors. These studies have been examined to determine whether there is evidence to support the five most quoted risk factors:

- Intra-individual dynamics (psychopathology of the abuser).
- Intergenerational transmission of violence (cycle of violence between generations).
- Dependency and exchange relationships between abuser and abused.
- Stress.
- Social isolation.

INTRA-INDIVIDUAL DYNAMICS

Evidence of either mental health problems or alcohol misuse on the part of the abuser was noted in four of the six case control studies considered. However this finding leads to further questions for the practitioner to consider rather than clarifying the situation:

- Does alcohol render individuals prone to inflicting abuse because it removes inhibitions and increases impulse responses, including aggression?
- Does prolonged alcoholism foster a dependency between adult children and their elderly parents, which distresses and disturbs both, leading to the occurrence of abuse?
- Do individuals with a tendency towards alcoholism increase their alcohol consumption in an attempt to cope when frustrated with elder care?

A further question must be asked, of course: for whom is the alcohol a problem?

INTERGENERATIONAL TRANSMISSION OF VIOLENCE

This risk factor was not verified in any of the six case control studies reviewed by Bennett *et al.* (1997). However it must be said that this factor is notoriously difficult to research. The intergenerational aspect suggests that extremely sensitive information about family relationships forms the basis of the research questions, yet it can be difficult to ask such questons with sufficient sensitivity. However some studies have successfully considered these issues. Several of the case control studies did detect evidence of longstanding abusive relationships. Furthermore the National Center on Elder Abuse (1998) has found that almost nine out of ten alleged abusers are related to the victims, according to both types of data source (APS and sentinels) used in the study.

DEPENDENCY

This risk factor has a lengthy history in the elder abuse debate. This is due in part to the view that decremental decline in old age results in dependency. Both academic gerontologists and older people themselves are rigorously challenging this view of continued deterioration.

Nevertheless it has appeal as a 'logical' explanation, especially within the welfare professions.

Social work and social care practitioners often work with and provide services for the most dependent older people in society. Practitioners become used to seeing 'problems' and tend to forget what 'normal ageing' consists of. One of the issues that needs clarification here is what we mean by 'dependency', and as importantly, dependency by whom and on whom. Certainly, within the case control studies the only evidence of dependency is that abused people are less impaired than non-abused individuals. Additionally, one study suggests that those who abuse are dependent on the abused people for finance and living arrangements. The direction and extent of any dependency is an important consideration in any assessment.

STRESS

This factor is similar to dependency. The stereotypical picture is of a younger carer (mostly daughters or daughters-in-law) caring for an ageing relative who is dependent upon her for help and support. Stress builds up and becomes unbearable for the carer, leading to abuse. Stress is a complex issue. Not only can it represent an internal reaction to circumstances but it can also result from external or internal pressures that become difficult or impossible to manage. Only one of the case control studies reported conclusively that stress is a factor. This was a Swedish study by Grafstrom *et al.* (1992). In this study the group of abusive carers reported worse health than might be expected. They also took higher levels of psychotropic medication than other groups (perhaps indicative of psychopathology). It may also be that the perception of whether a situation is stressful or not is important in the consideration of risk factors.

SOCIAL ISOLATION

Exclusion from wider community and/or family support and other social contacts may increase the likelihood of an abusive situation occuring, but the evidence for this is mixed. The longitudinal cohort study by Lachs *et al.* (1997) found that mistreated individuals are more likely to be living with someone, but they also have fewer social ties. The authors' explanation provides some support for a social isolation theory:

> *Our data provide some support for this theory as the number of social ties (measured by standardised social network instruments) was lower in mistreated subjects, yet 80 per cent of mistreated subjects lived with another party.* (ibid., 1997, p 474)

Perhaps the danger is of being in an abusive situation but socially isolated from family, friends and welfare agencies or other forms of community support.

Mental health, alcohol and/or substance misuse, a past history of violence or abuse, dependency, stress and isolation are important factors to consider in any comprehensive assessment. However it is not possible for practitioners confidently to predict levels of risk of abuse simply by identifying these factors alone.

EMERGING RISK FACTORS

There are series of factors that emerge from the work of both Lachs *et al.* (ibid.) and the National Center on Elder Abuse (1998). Lachs *et al.* suggest that 'poverty, minority status, functional disability, and worsening cognitive impairment were risk factors for reported elder mistreatment' (ibid., 1997, p 474). Worsening cognitive ability is also found to be a factor by the National Center on Elder Abuse (1998), whose findings indicate that older people who are unable to care for themselves, or are mentally confused or depressed, are especially vulnerable to abuse, neglect and self-neglect.

This implies that risk of abuse should be assessed at a number of levels. Structural factors, including environmental issues and social divisions, should be taken into account alongside particular family histories and individual characteristics.

RISK FACTORS FOR INSTITUTIONAL ABUSE

The risk factors considered above all relate to abuse in domiciliary situations. There are a series of risk factors connected, specifically to institutional abuse. However research in this area is even more limited and suffers similar inadequacies. There is a failure to disaggregate different forms of abuse (see Stevenson, 1999; Stanley *et al.* 1999). Furthermore it is often difficult to discover whether the causes of abuse are individual failings or structural aspects such as managerial weaknesses. The factors that are known include:

- Lack of staff training in and education on caring for elders.
- Work-related stress and professional burn-out.
- The social expectations imposed on a predominantly female, low-paid workforce.
- The personal psychopathology of individual staff members and residents.
- The personal characteristics of victims.
- Lack of adequate resources to provide good-quality care.

CONCLUSION

Whilst definitions remain problematic, certain signs of consensus are emerging. If we are not entirely clear about global definitions, we at least have a degree of consensus about the types of behaviour that constitute abuse and neglect. The caveat to the above statement must be that all the terms and definitions developed so far have been professionally constructed. In the UK we have yet to explore the use of such terms with older people and carers themselves. Social and health care practitioners must therefore beware of imposing definitions on situations without carefully examining their reasons for doing so as this could be potentially oppressive and abusive. Adopting a client-centred perspective, starting at the point of concern for the client, helps to ensure inclusion in the process and the debate and accords with social work and health care values.

Power and gender in elder abuse

INTRODUCTION

At first sight it may seem obvious and certainly uncontroversial that gender and power issues are central to elder abuse. However they interrelate in extremely complex ways. For instance we cannot blame one single aspect of gender or power relations for the development of violence and aggression between people. It is not enough to say that elder abuse is perpetrated by damaged, sick or stressed individuals or that attitudes that allow the continuation of elder abuse simply result from personal prejudice. Causative theories of elder abuse are not singular but interact in complex ways. We should consider the interplay of structural power relations throughout society as setting the context for abuse to be minimised, condoned or even perpetrated. By examining the organisational, agency and cultural factors that reflect social structures one may discover the ways in which the *status quo* is reinforced in respect of gender divided roles, work and status. The socialisation of individuals in families is determined by wider social structures and cultural factors, and in turn recreates them by joining in with the gender and power games promoted. All these factors interact to produce individual experiences and behaviours. Some of these are fundamentally abusive and outlawed by society, some are neither condoned nor proscribed, and some are perpetuated within the existing social fabric. This situation is often internalised by individuals, who add to the maintenance and development of a gendered and unequal society.

SOCIAL CARE – BETWEEN THE PUBLIC AND THE PRIVATE

In their protection work, social and health care practitioners also lend support and as such wield considerable power in the private world of families. Working to protect others entails the legitimate exercise of power in human situations. It is crucial to the professional development of practitioners that they attain an understanding of power in order to work within their 'protective responsibilities' (Stevenson and Parsloe, 1993). A large degree of this power derives from the legislative base to their work but they also have personal power in the eyes of those with whom they work: often the dispossessed, disenfranchised and vulnerable. However, not only do practitioners exercise power, they are also subject to power – the power of their agency, the state and legislation. Service users may exercise a certain degree of power in their interactions with practitioners by *resistance*. They may choose or refuse services; they may challenge or resist the protective practices of social and health care workers. Power can be understood as a process in which we all engage as professionals and individuals. It is communicated by interaction between those who control and those who are controlled. Varying degrees of power are held by the participants in a social event. This is no less the case when social and health care professionals meet with service users.

A referral was received concerning Mrs Green, whose memory was causing her neighbours and her daughter some worries. A social worker arranged with Mrs Green's daughter to visit and assess the situation. Mrs Green decided the visit was stuff and nonsense and refused to let the social worker in. Mrs Green's daughter made an official complaint to the social worker's team manager and the local councillor serving the area. She demanded that action be taken to protect her vulnerable mother, and found it difficult to acknowledge that her mother had the right to refuse entry or offers of assistance. (author's case study)

Because power is interactive the outcome of any interaction between people is unpredictable. Power can produce positive changes as well as feel repressive. Wherever there is power, there is resistance. Two types of resistance have been identified. One type is used to justify the expression of further power and restriction. The second type, on the other hand, is successful in bringing about intended changes. Power can be understood as being constantly expressed in daily life to shape and control people's experiences. In this sense power operates

at the everyday level in social practice – at the poin...
is said and what is done.

GENDER, POWER AND ELDER ABUSE

Sexism does not refer solely to the prejudice expressed by
individual males. It also results from the social structures
developed to perpetuate a gendered ordering of society. It
includes the ways in which agencies and organisations
reflect this order and impose normative roles and
expectations on members. Sexism and the unequal
distribution of power and roles in society can be linked to
other forms of oppression, leading to the necessity for a
gender–power analysis that places gender within a wider
social and political context. For instance child care is seen
as the legitimate role of women, as are care in the
community and low-paid care jobs in residential homes.
Older women are marginalised in society on the grounds of
both gender and age. The negative connotations of ageism
and ideas of dependency and disability aggregate in the
negotiations of power in society.

The domestic violence approach to elder abuse
emphasises power imbalances and highlights the position of
victimised groups in society. Maintaining a clear distinction
between victim and perpetrator is not always possible with
this approach. This is demonstrated in the *conflict tactics
approach* which sees conflict as constructed and maintained
by both parties. A corrective to this approach is provided by
the 'domination' model of domestic violence, which focuses
on the power of male aggressors over women rather than the
sharing of responsibility between them.

The family violence model has been developed further in
Bennett *et al.* (1997). Family violence can be understood as
violence that occurs within families against the powerless
and vulnerable, usually women, and in the context of elder
abuse, older women. It is an aggressive act by a more
powerful individual, group or institution against someone
with less power. The power imbalance may not necessarily
be at the conscious level. It develops from the patterns of
interaction between individuals from which the relative
power positions are secured. In these ways the family
violence approach fits the personal, cultural and structural
model of oppression (Thompson, 1998).

Both of the above approaches to elder abuse focus on physical violence as the central theme. This may lead to reduced recognition of other forms of abuse and neglect. The figures available suggest that women are more likely to be victims and men are more likely to be abusers, but these figures are only marginally higher than would be expected on the basis of the proportion of female elders in the general population. If it is true that violence by women towards men is greatly underreported, the link between gender and elder abuse is less strong.

Barnett *et al.* (1997) review research on the characteristics of those who abuse and those who are abused. The results regarding gender are contradictory. In the United States, APS figures reveal that most victims are female (68 per cent). In an earlier survey in Boston it was found that the majority of victims were male (52 per cent), whilst 65 per cent of people responding to the survey were female. According to this study, the victimisation rate for men (5.1 per cent) is double that for women (2.5 per cent) and yet the population over 60 years of age is disproportionately female.

However it is recognised that women tend to suffer more serious abuse and injuries than men. This may mean that women are more likely to come to the attention of health and social care agencies because of their injuries. Males are more likely to be violent and to commit more serious violence than females. Research indicates that males are more likely to use physical violence whilst females are more likely to be neglectful.

Eileen and Ken Royle had lived together for forty-five years. Eileen was a small woman who had frequently been on the receiving end of Ken's fists. As he became older and frailer Eileen had to take on more of the physical and daily care he needed. She took to this with a sense of duty at first, but soon began to leave him unattended for long period in his unheated room, and provided him with small, insubstantial meals. When her son challenged her about the health of his father, Eileen replied 'I've had forty-five years of him. Now it's my turn.' (author's case study)

Men are more likely to live with someone else, which may make abuse more likely. This corresponds with research into the characteristics and profiles of abusers: frequently a relative who has lived with the victim for a long time, usually an adult child, the spouse, a grandchild, a sibling or another relative. Abuse by non-family members is comparatively rare: abuse is mainly spousal.

Historically, elder abuse in domestic settings has been constructed as a problem between a female abuser and an elderly parent – often the mother – within a caring context. Aitken's Northamptonshire study found, however, that elderly females tend to be abused by sons rather than husbands or daughters (Aitken and Griffin, 1996). The women in this study were physically abused, the men were psychologically abused. This perhaps reflects gendered behaviour. There are frequent references in the literature to 'dysfunctional families'. This creates the view that elder abuse is a symptom of a poorly functioning family, and therefore gender issues are not brought into the debate.

INTRODUCING A FEMINIST PERSPECTIVE

Aitken and Griffin (1996), writing from a feminist perspective, suggest that elder abuse should be treated as a category of domestic violence, but should emphasise a gender–power analysis:

> *the relationship between elder abuse and care and between elder abuse and family violence needs to be revisited. Neither care nor family violence by itself offers a sufficient explanation for elder abuse; a more over-arching way of thinking about elder abuse which would also allow an appropriate integration of gender issues would be in terms of power and dependency.* (ibid., p 139).

In situations of elder abuse there is likely to be a combination of complex sociological and psychological factors operating at and between the structural, organisational, family and individual levels. Feminist perspectives focus on the role of gender and power within domestic violence. Social, political and economic processes are seen as supporting patriarchy in the subjugation of women. Violence is a means men use to maintain their position of power at the societal, family and interpersonal levels. A range of causal factors must be considered and individual differences and diversity recognised. The additional variable of age must be taken into account when discussing elder abuse.

Whittaker (1995) believes that interest in elder abuse has developed within the context of domestic violence and child abuse. The growth of interest in all three areas has shared a number of common features: slow recognition and acceptance; difficulties with definitions and concepts; and an emphasis on stress and pathology as opposed to gender/power and male violence. Whittaker argues that research and theory construction in the field of elder abuse has occurred in a socio-political climate that privileges studies on definition and prevalence above the gender debate. The main ungendered approaches she identifies include:

- Situational stress, with a focus on 'victims' and underpinned by stereotypical notions of ageing and dependency.
- Pathology of abusers, which considers a range of predisposing factors.
- Family violence, which reflects the intention to safeguard 'normal' family relationships.

Accusingly, she states:

There appears to be no attempt to include the victim's subjective experience of abuse as part of the definitional debate and very little attention is paid to issues of inequality of power between victim and perpetrator other than to stress that old women are not children and that dependency exists as a two-way process within relationships and between them and their abusers (Whittaker, 1996, p 149).

The power of language is important. The change in terminology from 'granny bashing' to 'elder abuse' may mask the gender specificity of abuse. It cannot simply be construed as a move away from the use of stigmatising and patronising language. We must also recognise the homogenisation of older people within research, which

takes no account of difference, especially in respect of
gender differences.

TOWARDS A GENDERED ANALYSIS OF ELDER ABUSE

Feminist theories of elder abuse have moved beyond the
health and welfare debate to a theory in which age and
gender and the relationship between them and other social
divisions is given equal importance. The potential for
violence and abuse is fundamental to gender and power in
all social relationships.

> *A feminist analysis of elder abuse, whilst recognising
> the gendered nature of inequality, would have to
> acknowledge women's capacity for violence and
> recognise that the issue of power is more problematic
> and less fixed than previously imagined. The
> connections between relations of age, gender and power
> would be central categories of analysis and the notion
> of power would require a different treatment.
> This means treating power like age and gender relations
> as something fluid, rather than fixed and monolithic, as
> something which varies according to what it is in
> relation to or with* (Whittaker, 1995, p 152).

There is generally a lack of feminist critiques of elder
abuse although gender relations have been seen as central to
examinations of the physical abuse of children. The concept
of domination rather than power has been employed to
demonstrate its significance. Research on domestic violence
and the development of interagency working lays emphasis
on domestic violence towards adult women and children.
Older women are not specifically included, although the
research does not explicitly exclude them (Hague and Malos,
1998). There is, however, a marginalisation of older people
and an uncritical reinforcement of hierarchies of concern
that reflects socio-cultural power relations. Whittaker (1996)
advocates a methodology of inclusion in participative
research on elder abuse, which, she states, cannot be
divorced from its social context and the patriarchal rather
than the pathological family. It is here, perhaps, that social
work and health care practitioners can contribute to the
debate. The understandings gained from practice inform the

need to develop social work and health care that emphasise the social positions, divisions and possibilities of those involved.

Feminist analyses start with gender. The marginalisation of older people, and in particular older women, in society is taken into account. In the patriarchal context, men are seen as having access to greater power over the more vulnerable and less powerful and being protected by societal norms. It is therefore possible to understand the allegedly controlling characteristics and behaviours of non-compliant, dependent victims as a struggle and resistance against oppression and male control. This represents a move away from explanations based on caregiver stress that absolve the perpetrator of responsibility.

Alice Jones was blamed by her husband for 'spoiling our retirement'– a year after Fred Jones had retired she had become frail, increasingly tired and wanted to stay at home more. He asked for help to 'make her like she used to be'.

It was clear that Jack was experiencing a degree of physical stress and strain in looking after the house and Alice. He was also emotionally concerned for her. However it became clear that he wanted Alice to return to her former self – doing what he wanted and participating in activities he was interested in. When Alice was asked what she wanted for herself he banned the social worker from his house and stopped Alice from attending a day centre she had begun to enjoy.
(author's case study)

It has been suggested that feminist theory presents an analysis of only one type of violence and victimisation and that it does not account for child abuse, sibling abuse, violence by women or the abuse of older people. However, this view is fundamentally flawed since it depicts feminism as representing only a single approach, whereas there are in fact great differences and divergences that characterise the many types of feminism.

When gender is seen as a constructed socio-cultural process, rather than biologically determined as 'sex', it is no longer enough to consider that males are violent and women are peaceful and nurturing. The constructivist approach highlights diversity and rejects the attempt to define one sole cause of women's oppression.

There are proportionately more women than men in the general population the older the population becomes. Ageism, sexism and structural divisions combine to create power imbalances by insisting on women's inferior status and thereby facilitating and exacerbating abuse. Thus our understanding of abuse as social work and health care professionals acknowledges that society, organisations and agencies contribute to the abuse experienced by older people. This provides the rationale to work for change at the three levels of prevention highlighted in the introduction.

Elder abuse, however, cannot be seen solely within the context of families and interpersonal relationships. The fluid nature of power and the continuing prevalence of patriarchal assumptions is linked to abuse within the context of health and social care. In the contemporary demographic situation. There are increasingly higher numbers of women at the top end of the age range. Women tend to be poorer, which affects their choices. The health needs of older women are not considered in public policies, and poverty and ill-health foster dependency and exploitation. Added to this is the fact that many women live alone and social services departments target single people rather than couples. Also, it is not only those who receive care who are marginalised. Middle-aged women undertake the bulk of informal care. Many of these women have just relinquished the responsibility of caring for their children and will be employed too.

It is acknowledged that the social and health care agencies charged with 'protective responsibility' may overtly or inadvertently abuse. Jack (1994) states that dependence, power and violation represent the currency of relationships and that mutual (albeit unequal) dependency, powerlessness and violation foster abuse by formal carers.

The function of caring has been professionalised in health and welfare and is conceptualised as women's work (Jack, 1994). The term 'social iatrogenesis' has been coined to refer to the ways in which the organisation of care practices could lead to ill-health by increasing stress and bureaucratising care. The social organisation of social and health care continues this process. Older people receive ameliorative or palliative care rather than curative treatment. This may be doubly stigmatising because a potentially positive outcome is denied. The emphasis is on the outcome and content rather than the process.

> *The recognition of the powerlessness shared by old women and their female carers as a result of the combination of ageism and sexism within the professionalization of welfare, leads to new perspectives on abuse by formal carers, perceiving abuser and abused as powerless socially, organisationally and personally, locked together in a relationship of mutual, enforced dependency. The medium through which this socially-constructed powerlessness becomes the individual and collective abuse of elderly people takes place is the 'exchange relationship' of formal care* (Jack, 1994, p 79).

Exchange theory states that individuals act according to the real and perceived benefits and costs of continuing a relationship. Within this, the most dependent is the least powerful. Those with greater power seek to maximise gains and minimise the contributions to be made to a relationship. The person cared for may be seen as an inconvenience and in this way a subculture of abuse may arise. Jack (ibid.) uses Seligman's concept of 'learned helplessness' to show that ageist stereotypes of dependence and increasing incompetence lead to the erosion of personal control in the context of formal care. Perceived powerlessness and dependency have been implicated in abusers in formal and informal settings.

Women carers predominate in the workforce and the work is consequently devalued. Women who are cared for are also discriminated against. Jack (ibid. p 89) states: '. . . in order to ensure her dependency-needs are met, the old woman is compelled to surrender her claim to adult status to the female carer, whose limited status within the organisation depends on her complete possession of the caring role'.

Maria Beadle was 103 years old. She had never married, had worked as a school teacher until her retirement and had moved into residential care after the death of her sister 13 years earlier. The staff were disgusted at her recent 'depraved activity'. They took to giving her cold baths and a rough towel drying whilst leaving her in her room for long periods and making extremely abusive comments to her about her behaviour. In fact, she had learned to masturbate in the privacy of her own room and had been caught doing so by one of the night care staff, who organised a campaign to 'stamp out this behaviour'. (author's case study)

The development of continual assessment for service users and staff development may engender feelings of continued surveillance, of not being able to escape or resist effectively. It therefore sets the scene for the creation and maintenance of dependence and marginalisation by encouraging learned helplessness and submission to the power of surveillance. Disciplinary practices contribute to the operation of power through such techniques as visibility, residential designs aimed at maximum surveillance, and the processing, filing and creation of individual 'cases'. Further divisions are created by binary distinctions such as practitioner and client, old and young, healthy and unhealthy, abuser and abused, and individuals begin to watch over themselves.

It is the social organisation of gender that allocates roles and meaning and contributes to the marginalisation of elder abuse at the social, agency and personal level. As Thompson (1998) states in respect of antidiscriminatory practice, those who are not actively seeking to change this state of affairs are part of the problem. It is therefore the responsibility of social and health care practitioners to acknowledge their own assumptions and gendered positions. We must also work within our agencies to develop an approach that recognises the importance of gender and power relations. We need to influence those who set the terms of the argument at the policy-making level. As Kaufman (1994, p. 146) states 'we all experience power in diverse ways, some that celebrate life and diversity and others that hinge on control and domination'. A gender–power analysis can be used to develop approaches that celebrate life and diversity in our attempt to deal with elder abuse.

Assessment, vulnerability and protection in elder abuse

INTRODUCTION: THE CONTEXT OF ASSESSMENT

Assessment in situations of potential elder abuse is a fundamental activity helps to identify the needs, risks and issues to be worked with. It also helps the practitioner to begin to develop a care plan and interventions to reduce the risk of further abuse. The tasks of the social work practitioner include developing a constructive working relationship, making an assessment and, subsequent to this, care planning and seeing to the provision of appropriate services.

Prior to any active intervention there must be a clear period of assessment and evaluation (Lithwick, 1999). This will follow the particular laws of the country and the policies and procedures designed to deal with elder abuse within the agency in question. This is no less the case in the UK. Assessment may involve the use of a range of screening instruments designed for working in the context of elder abuse (see appendix 3.1), but should always include information on:

- Evidence of abuse and/or neglect.
- The immediacy of the danger.
- Past history of abuse/neglect in the family.
- Attempts by the family to resolve problems – success and barriers.
- The older person's feelings about the situation.
- The older person's goals in resolving the conflict.
- The ability of the older person to make decisions and understand the consequences.
- The ability of the older person to protect her- or himself.

Health and social care workers in the UK operate within the context of care management. In terms of legislation, social workers in particular are bound by the National Health Service and Community Care Act, 1990, especially Section 47, where the assessment role is clearly stated.

At the heart of community care assessment is the concept of 'need'. This is a difficult term to define, and to a large extent it is left to each local authority to determine in the light of their resources and policies. Mandelstam (1999) asks whether it is 'needs-for-services' or 'needs in the abstract' that should be assessed because of the discrepancies between legislation and government guidance. Also, questions of eligibility criteria further confound the matter of who will receive a service. The move towards needs-led assessment has been welcomed in principle by many social workers. However, the Community Care Act talks about 'needs for services' rather than needs in a more abstract sense (section 47.1a). Also, principles of fairness might demand that assessment takes into account the available services and resources so as to enable full participation in the assessment. Guidance from the Social Services Inspectorate for England and Wales, concerning implementation of the community care reforms, implored practitioners to assess the needs of individuals (and in particular their social care needs) rather than assess the need for service provision and specific services (Social Services Inspectorate, 1991a, 1991b).

Community care assessment, undertaken by social workers, is a statutory duty but also a service in its own right. If the assessment indicates a need for services the decision to provide these is a separate duty. The form the assessment should take is also left up to the local authorities to determine. In some cases this has led to rigid assessments based on a single event and employing rigid criteria.

> *Where it appears to a local authority that any person for whom they may provide or arrange for the provision of community care services may be in need of any such services, the authority . . . shall carry out an assessment of his needs for those services; and . . . having regard to the results of that assessment, shall then decide whether his needs call for the provision by them of any such services* (National Health Service and Community Care Act, 1990, section 47 (1)).

The Social Services Inspectorate document *No Longer Afraid* (1993), which concerns elder abuse and neglect, includes the clear statement that the protection of vulnerable elders should not be viewed or treated in isolation from the wider processes of assessment and care management. This is very much within the framework contained in documents relating to assessment and care management (Social Services Inspectorate, 1991a,b). The guide developed for practitioners suggests that decisions concerning the assessment (either simple or complex) should consist of a consideration of the following areas:

- The nature of the presenting problem.
- The purpose of the intervention.
- Urgency or risk.
- Preferred solutions.
- Special requirements.

Some of these may need to be part of the full assessment process, however! When considering such aspects as eligibility criteria for assessment and then for service, there are further factors that need to be taken into account. In addition to negotiations about the scope of the assessment, there is a need to choose the setting of the assessment with some care; a need to clarify expectations, agree objectives and to establish a relationship of trust between practitioner and potential service user. This should also promote the possibility of working in partnership with the individuals concerned and allow for the setting of priorities (ibid)

The community care process consists of two stages. First there is an assessment of the need for services and then a decision about which services will be provided. The decision about services depends on the rationing process effected by the setting of eligibility criteria. It is within this context that social workers first come into contact with elder abuse and begin to assess needs.

LEAD ASSESSORS
It is, of course, important that one person should take a lead role in the assessment process. This includes taking

responsibility for the coordination of the specific assessment of possible abuse. Social workers are often ideally placed to do this, particularly in relation to their role as care managers and assessors of need and risk. However this may not always be the case, particularly within the setting of a multidisciplinary team, such as may be found in some hospitals specialising in the care of older people. In such settings, other members of the team might be as well if not better placed to take such a role. It is therefore necessary to decide at an early stage who the lead individual and the lead agency will be. Government guidance indicates that every agency must have a designated lead officer for work that relates to the protection of vulnerable adults, including of course older people (Department of Health, 2000).

The choice of lead person in any assessment of abuse may be influenced by other factors such as which agency received the original referral, and policy statements on procedures for protection in terms of which agency carries overall responsibility within a particular setting or locality. However local authorities have the lead responsibility for overall coordination of multi-agency arrangements for the protection of vulnerable adults (ibid.)

OBJECTIVES OF ASSESSMENT IN ELDER ABUSE

Whilst the overall goal of assessment and intervention is to stop the abuse, there are specific objectives relevant to each individual and situation. Assessment processes are likely to vary between practitioners and in ideal circumstances should encompass a multidisciplinary approach. Within an holistic assessment of individuals and their needs there should be consideration of the potential for contributions by other professionals. A multidisciplinary assessment may be the best way of achieving this, rather than a number of separate individual assessments by various professionals. Such contributions could include comments and observations by representatives of several disciplines, for example nurses, doctors, occupational therapists, physiotherapists, speech and language therapists, dieticians, dentists, organisers of voluntary groups and so forth. It is important to bear in mind that as each situation of abuse is different, the number of relevant contributions from others will vary. It is essential that these should be relevant and meaningful to the individual and their circumstances rather than a prescribed number of contributions from a set number of professionals irrespective of the needs and circumstances of the individual. The added importance is that other professionals may be able to contribute to a fuller understanding of potentially abusive situations and add to the overall understanding of usual and preferred lifestyles. Ideally, as with child protection, skilled and qualified practitioners should undertake the most complex and difficult assessment work. Even at its most basic level, the assessment process should include consideration of the following:

- What are the main concerns, issues, problems and needs?
- What are the priority areas?
- Who are the key parties involved?
- Why have the difficulties developed (Sutton, 1994)

Middleton (1997) suggests that the process of assessment consists of four distinct parts: establishing a working relationship, data collection (information gathering), analysis (of the different options available, including the risks associated with these) and planning. It is possible to break each of these areas down further, and this is achieved in Middleton's accessible text, which is recommended to readers. To give some idea of the range and scope of these areas, however, it is useful to consider just one: the need in the initial stage of relationship building to establish 'ground rules' with the service user. Middleton defines these as follows:

- The purpose of the assessment.
- How the assessment will be conducted.
- The length of the assessment.
- Who will contribute to it.
- Any special needs (advocates/interpreters).
- Methods of recording.
- Who has access to the results.
- Where the documentation will be kept.
- Possible outcomes.
- Limits to the assessment.
- Any rights to appeal.

It is apparent that in an assessment of alleged abuse or neglect (and 'assessment' is surely a preferable term to 'investigation', with it's quasi-legal connotations) some ground rules are likely to be more important than others, such as who will contribute to the assessment, who will have access to the results and where the relevant documents will be kept. It is very important to establish these rules with the individuals involved from the beginning of the assessment process.

It is possible that the assessor may be the only advocate for the rights of the person at the time of the assessment. The assessor should also take action to demystify the process by informing the individuals involved of what is happening or is likely to happen, and of any legal implications. Advice may also be given on contact with the police or gaining further legal guidance and assistance. In practice this may often be quite difficult as situations can be fraught and full of conflict or even danger, and people may not always listen to or be able to understand what is being communicated. It is possible, of course, that the ground rules will need to be revisited and reaffirmed with individuals at various points during the assessment.

Some further and specific areas for assessment in elder abuse are presented in box 3.1.

AREAS FOR ASSESSMENT

- The abuse (or abusive situation), including antecedents, consequences and likely future patterns.
- The individual's methods of dealing with the situation (including any ineffective coping strategies).
- Degrees of disability; the nature of any dependency (of abuser and abused person).
- Risk factors, including stressors, both internal and external to the situation.
- Family history, social context of the family and the dynamics of family relationships within the situation, including information on the balance of power and of communication systems and interactions.
- The views, beliefs and attitudes of key players in the situation as to the nature of the situation and likely outcomes.

▶

◀

- The views, beliefs and attitudes of key players within the situation in respect of the preferred outcomes.
- Consideration of the needs of all parties in the situation is likely to be crucial; it may not be appropriate or necessary to offer an abuser a separate assessment in every situation but this will require careful consideration; in any case an assessment of the distinctive needs of all parties will require integration into the overall assessment process.

(source Parker and Penhale, 1998, p. 178)

ENGAGING CLIENTS IN THE PROCESS

Social work and health care practitioners have long recognised that assessment is a dynamic and ongoing process and not simply the production of a time-specific report. It may take some time to conduct and complete even an initial assessment and the practitioner should be prepared for this. It is worth bearing in mind that in some respects an assessment is never complete, given the fluidity of many interpersonal situations. There may be an almost constant need to reassess as situations develop and alter. The active engagement of individuals in the narration of their story and their reality is a useful part of the assessment process.

As we have seen above, there are a number of factors that need to be taken into account as part of the assessment process. This is so for most, if not all, assessments. Assessment of particular abusive situations should be 'needs-led but *abuse focused*.' (Bennett *et al.*, 1997, p. 173).

The initial focus of any assessment must be the establishment of a clear working relationship, with social workers using their interpersonal skills to engage individuals and families where allegations of elder abuse have occurred.

SEEKING THE CLIENTS' VIEWS AND OFFERING CHOICE

When gathering preliminary information on elder abuse, social work's particular emphasis on values and ethics is brought into sharp relief. In order to make a comprehensive assessment, practitioners should offer people the opportunity to speak to them alone, and should seek to identify and clarify their views and wishes. Indeed there are those who advocate that the individual should always be seen separately from any carer or other person involved in the situation especially when potential abuse is involved. Whilst it is desirable to do this it may not always be possible particularly as the individual may not wish to be interviewed apart from others. This does not mean, however, that the person should not be given the choice! It is also generally appropriate to offer the opportunity for a separate discussion, in private, to others involved in the situation, including the person who is thought to have been responsible for the abuse. Obviously considerations of risk, danger and personal safety must be taken into account by the practitioner in such instances and an informed decision taken about the desirability (or otherwise) of doing so.

NEGOTIATION AND PARTICIPATION: EMPHASISING VALUES AND CHOICES

A focus on the need of the individual for protection during the assessment process and the subsequent care planning stage should not serve to hamper the empowerment of the individual. Rather the focus should be on the individuals concerned, the abusive situation (or allegation) and the factors and circumstances that are contributing to the situation. A full assessment of needs, including safety, protection and assistance and how best to meet them, is an essential part of the process. Training courses for professionals are increasingly beginning to concentrate on such areas in order to assist with appropriate training in assessment and intervention skills. Further development is also necessary in the assessment of risk and danger as a crucial part of the process.

One of the most crucial matters for professionals to deal with is achieving and maintaining a balance between the protection of the individual and the right to self-determination. The principal assessor also needs to ensure that the design of the intervention is the most appropriate possible for the person in question (see Chapter 4). Within the context of assessment, however, it is important to remember that older people have the right in most cases to be autonomous. It is quite possible for professionals to work with individuals to determine their needs and suggest appropriate treatment options but for these individuals to refuse such offers.

The right of people to take their own decisions and risks needs to be closely linked to questions of capacity. This is also the case in respect of older people. If a person has capacity – which may defined as the ability to make informed choices and undertake actions subsequent to these choices – and declines assistance, this will limit the actions that can be taken. In terms of vulnerability and/or abuse, this may prevent social workers and other helping practitioners from acting in a protective way. Some guidelines may indicate that protection is necessary when capacity is limited or impaired, or, if a life-threatening situation ensues. Clear government advice is provided in the following quotation from *No Secrets*, and also in earlier guidance (Lord Chancellor's Department, 1999):

> *In order to make sound decisions, the vulnerable adult's emotional, physical, intellectual and mental capacity in relation to self-determination and consent and any intimidation, misuse of authority or undue influence will have to be assessed*
> **(Department of Health, 2000, 6.21).**

EXPLORING THE RELATIONSHIP

In order to gain as full a view of the situation as possible, it is usually necessary to interview the individuals involved together. This serves to provide indicators of the nature and quality of the relationship and interaction between the individuals involved. What will need to be determined as far as possible beforehand is the degree of potential risk and danger in conducting joint interviews. Here too, related issues of individual safety for the older person and also for the practitioner need to be considered. It may be that the involvement of several practitioners (or a line manager) in a potentially dangerous situation will be necessary in order to ensure adequate protection for the individuals concerned. Thus careful planning of the assessment process is a necessary prerequisite and assistance with this from a specialist practitioner/consultant or line manager is recommended. This may take the form of close liaison with the lead officer in the agency.

Tanya, a social worker in an adult care team, had been asked to visit Amy Kitchen by her daughter, Tilly, who was concerned that her mother was unable to make a drink or something to eat whilst her son was at work. She was also concerned that Jack Kitchen, Amy's son, was keeping her locked in the house because he was afraid she would wander off and get lost. Amy had been diagnosed with dementia the previous year after the sudden death of her husband. Tilly said she could not visit her mother because she was afraid of her brother, who had threatened her with violence if she did so. This situation had arisen after Tilly had contacted her mother's doctor, who had initiated an approved social work assessment some three months ago. The assessment had not resulted in admission to hospital but services had been suggested to assist with Amy's care when Jack was at work. He had refused these services.

Tanya discussed her concerns with her team manager. It was highlighted that it was Jack who had refused the services and that Amy had not been consulted. Tilly's worries were acknowledged, although it was clear that no actual violence had occurred. The team manager and Tanya decided to involve the GP who had initiated the approved social work assessment. Amy's doctor suggested that Jack was a 'very demonstrative and forceful man but not a risk to anyone', but she was concerned for Amy's well-being. She felt that Amy could no longer make decisions on her own.

Armed with this knowledge, Tanya and her manager constructed a plan for an interview that would involve both Jack and his mother but would allow each of them to be spoken to individually. The team manager would visit with Tanya and their concerns would be presented in a way that invited solutions and included both Jack and his mother in searching for these.

Taking family system/social networks and relationships into account

The process of assessment requires information to be collected from key individuals. For many people, the support derived from their families and wider social networks provides an effective buffer against problematic situations and unwanted interference. It is necessary, therefore, to consider the role and extent of such relationships as part of the assessment.

This of course necessitates a wide perspective that includes the views, perceptions and wishes of family members and other significant people in the life of the person being assessed. In addition to basic assessment questions, the following may be of particular importance when considering situations of potential or likely abuse (Social Services Inspectorate, 1995)

- Where did the concerns arise ?
- Why are they being raised now?
- What action (if any) does the referrer expect to happen?
- Does the vulnerable person/carer know about the referral and the concern?
- Is there a need for an advocate for the older person?
- What is the likely outcome if assistance is refused?
- What safeguards need to be established within the situation?

It is through attention to detail in the gathering of information on these questions from a wide range of sources that the assessment of relationships can be successfully completed.

Care-giving, stress and assessment

Since the early 1980s much has been researched and written about the stress and burden engendered by care-giving, especially in relation to family and friends but also more recently in relation to social care staff. Explorations of the satisfaction and positive aspects of caring have been fewer (Nolan, 1999) but are nonetheless important. It may be preferable, in relation to assessments, for the practitioner to consider the nature and quality of the care-giving experience for the carer and the care recipient. This can help avoid particular attitudes and preconceptions by practitioners that might be conveyed to service users during contact with them. It is also important for practitioners to be aware of research on caregivers' perception of degrees of stress. Research undertaken in the United States suggests that the perception of the situation by the caregiver as stressful appears to correlate with the existence of abusive situations, rather than stress *per se*. To expand briefly, if situations that appear to an objective, external observer to be unlikely to produce high levels of stress are nonetheless perceived as stressful by the caregiver, then high levels of stress are likely to be experienced by the caregiver. Abusive situations may well then develop and be maintained. We must also be mindful, however, that whilst stress may indeed contribute to the development and continuation of some abusive situations, it appears insufficient, in isolation, to provide a satisfactory explanation for the majority of situations of elder abuse and neglect.

EXPLORING RISKS AND DANGERS

On the basis of information gathered, the practitioner needs to consider wider issues of risk and danger, such as whether those involved pose a danger to themselves or others by their actions or lack of actions. When assessing the likely risk to self and others the assessor (and indeed all those involved in the assessment) should take the following into consideration:

- The reliability of the evidence of risk.
- Relevant past history and past behaviour.
- The degree of likely risk and its nature.
- The willingness and ability to cope of those with whom the individual lives.
- Any misunderstandings that may arise from assumptions based on gender and power relations, given the importance of these issues in cases of elder abuse.
- Any further misunderstandings based on social and cultural background, ethnic origin and other medical or health conditions, including deafness and other sensory impairments.

A number of inquiries into mental health tragedies have recommended that accurate details of all violent incidents be included in individuals' case records. Although this suggestion has largely been made in relation to younger adults with severe mental health difficulties, there is relevance here for older people. The need for clear, concise and accurate recording is essential in this context. Violent incidents do not just refer to acts committed by the individual in receipt of care, although of course an older person may react violently in certain situations. Acts of violence towards that person also need to be detailed, together with information on whether the violence has been confirmed, and by whom, or whether it remains at the level of suspicion. It is crucial that the views of the individuals involved are recorded as accurately as possible, including their views on the violence or abuse, the abusive situation and what the person might wish to happen within or about that situation. This may help to prevent misunderstandings in the future.

In addition, recommendations have been made that every professional working with mentally ill people who pose a risk of violence should have training in the assessment of dangerousness (Parsloe, 1999). This is of relevance to considerations of abuse and protection, for although older victims may not themselves pose risk of violence, the risk to them from others needs to be accurately documented as well as the risk to any others involved. For example the risk of violence towards care workers and other professionals must be taken into account and fully documented. In recent years many social services departments have developed policies on and procedures for (1) the assessment and management of risk and danger and (2) responding to the abuse of vulnerable adults. Any actions taken by a practitioner should, of course, be in accordance with any such departmental guidelines and procedures.

CONSIDER THE IMPORTANCE OF CHARACTERISTICS AND RISK FACTORS

In chapter 1 we reviewed potential risk factors for elder abuse and advocated caution in applying these. However any comprehensive assessment will take a range of risk factors into account. In terms of possible causative factors, it appears unlikely that any one factor alone causes abuse, rather there is an interplay between a number of different factors. There are many possible reasons why abuse happens, and the following may be involved in the development of abusive situations:

- A long-standing history of poor relationships within the family.
- The dependency of the abuser on the victim for finance, accommodation and transport or emotional support.
- The abuser having a history of mental health problems or a substance abuse problem.
- A pre-existing pattern of family violence (intergenerational transmission of violence).
- The social isolation of the victim and the abuser .

Additional risk factors might include the inability of a carer to care for the older person; other causes of stress such as unemployment, insufficient finance, and overcrowding; and/or inadequate systems of social support. Assessors need to develop their skills in asking sensitive questions about abuse and risk factors. Such factors should be addressed in training programmes for practitioners.

Assessing the Risks as an Aid to Protection

Although each case is unique in its own right, research evidence suggests certain general characteristics that need to be taken into account when assessing the need for protection or the risk of future harm. A safety or lethality assessment, followed by a full family history and assessment of the person's developmental level is important (Barnett *et al.*, 1997). Such an assessment would identify the trigger events and the history of the abuse, and the potential for resolution. Assessment should not just be concerned with the identification of problems, risks and areas of difficulty. It should also take into account the strengths of the individuals concerned and their ability to cope with and manage obstacles.

The characteristics to be considered include the potential for violence occurring within a situation, the ability of individuals to protect themselves and others included in the situation, and coping strategies. Structural factors such as age, gender, disability and health status, housing, occupation and finance, social support and isolation also need to be taken into account. Additionally, the use and abuse of alcohol and other substances and most importantly, whether there is a previous history of violence need to be established.

Other factors to be aware of include witnessing family violence, being brought up in a home where violence was the preferred way of dealing with conflict and previous occurrences of abuse. Care has to be taken with these, however, since many violent people share none of these characteristics and many who have had such experiences do not become abusers themselves. A high degree of discord in relationships is, perhaps understandably, found in many situations of violence in domestic settings. This can include difficulties in communication that may often be hostile, manipulative and demonstrate a failure to express love. Insecurity and emotional dependence may also be expressed within such relationships.

ASSESSMENT OF VULNERABLE PEOPLE UNDER THE MENTAL HEALTH ACT 1983

Some assessments of elder abuse take place within the framework of mental health legislation. In order to undertake comprehensive and effective assessments under the Mental Health Act, 1983, the assessor should have undergone a period of qualifying training. It is desirable, although not yet essential that the individual should also have had a substantial amount of experience in working with vulnerable adults and/or older people since their qualifying training. When assessing potential elder abuse under the Mental Health Act, 1983 it is essential that practitioners keep firmly in mind the needs and rights of those involved. *Is the assessment protective of the abused person or is it potentially abusive in itself?*

Individuals being assessed for compulsory admission to hospital or a guardianship order must be interviewed 'in a suitable manner' (as laid down in Section 13(2) of the Mental Health Act, 1983). This means that the person conducting the assessment must take any special needs into account, including those relating to communication and/or the language spoken by the individual. When working with older adults with dementia, for example, special care should be taken to ensure their views are elicited as far as practically possible. When undertaking a mental health assessment of an older person from an ethnic minority group it may be necessary to use an interpreter or to engage a practitioner with inside knowledge of cultural issues. In the majority of circumstances, but particularly in relation to allegations of abuse, the interpreter should not be a family member or a close significant person. It is of course important for practitioners to enquire sensitively about cultural issues that may affect the assessment and have a bearing on the person's needs. In addition, an assessment that includes issues relating to safety and protection requires information on the views and wishes of a wide variety of relevant people, including relatives, friends and professionals. The person's family and social network should be contacted to gain a full picture of that person in his or her local context.

Overall coordination of an assessment under the Mental Health Act, 1983 remains the responsibility of the principal assessor, (an approved social worker), a responsibility that is seen to befit the social work role in elder abuse (Department of Health, 2000).

The code of practice for the Mental Health Act, 1983 details the duties and good practice involved in making an assessment. These guidelines provide practice benchmarks and could be adapted to other assessment situations, for instance in relation to the assessment of an older person who may be in need of protection they could be amended as follows:

- Taking all relevant factors into account.
- Considering and where possible implementing appropriate alternatives to institutional care.
- Complying with any relevant legal requirements.

USING ASSESSMENT KNOWLEDGE TO PLAN

Whatever the particular context of the assessment it is crucial for practitioners to keep in mind that a key purpose of assessment is to gather information that will enable the meeting of identified needs to be planned. In this context, it is important to try to identify the primary or main cause of the abuse so that appropriate interventions can be offered later. For instance if the abuse is principally due to the stress of caregiving, then the provision of services within the community may be appropriate in order to alleviate or monitor the situation. If, however, the abuse is a result of the psychopathology of the abuser, then an approach that provides for treatment of the abuser (for example treatment for substance misuse) and protection of the older person is more likely to be required. A key part of the assessment at this stage is consideration of alternative strategies of intervention and the impact these might have. This has to be balanced against the pressures and strain on carers and their wider social networks.

The willingness of the parties to engage in assessment and intervention is of major importance here. Successful negotiation by the practitioner of the boundary between the private and public worlds of individuals is likely to be of significance in determining the outcome of the intervention as well as the assessment. If an individual is willing to participate in an assessment and subsequent intervention in order to resolve the problem (which will move the problem from the private to the public sphere) then the outcome is far more likely to be successful. It is important to be aware of the range and diversity of family forms and different cultural values and practices in the assessment of and intervention in violence and abuse.

The formulation of a care plan follows the completion of the initial assessment. It is at this point that assessment merges with the active intervention phase. In cases of elder abuse the care plan should reflect considerations of and strategies for future safety. According to the DoH guidance, 'Once the facts have been established an assessment of the needs of the adult abused will need to be made. This will entail joint discussion, decision and planning for the person's future protection' (Department of Health, 2000, 6.19). The care plan should include the following information:

- A statement on the key issues and risk areas.
- A statement of needs.
- Specific details of the safety plan (including emergency measures). ▶

◀

- The people and agencies involved in the delivery of the safety plan.
- The services to be provided.
- Review, monitoring and evaluation processes.

CONCLUSION

In this chapter we have explored a comprehensive assessment process that takes into account the views and wishes of all parties concerned in the assessment but especially the person who is the focus. The value base of social and health work is fundamental to good assessment practice. Negotiation and participation in assessment is encouraged. Also, when assessing elder abuse attention needs to be paid to risk assessment and risk management. This calls, as we have stressed throughout, for a coordinated response, that is multidisciplinary in nature.

There are many different and varied approaches to the assessment of situations of elder abuse. The method decided upon will of course depend on the overall context, the role and function of the practitioner and any agency requirements. Whatever approach is taken, it is essential that practitioners bear in mind the following key points:

- Engage the clients in the process.
- Seek the clients' views and offer choices as appropriate.
- Encourage negotiation and participation: emphasising values and choices.
- Explore the relationship between key people.
- Take the family system/social networks and relationships into account.
- Explore the possible risks and dangers.
- Consider the importance of characteristics and risk factors.
- Assess the risks identified as an aid to protection.
- Use the knowledge gained during the assessment to plan and establish a safety mechanism where necessary

The purpose of gaining a full picture of a situation, the impact on those involved and the wants and wishes of the individuals affected is to plan, develop and implement interventions that will result in change. In the next chapter we shall consider ways in which practitioners can work with those who have been abused and those who abuse.

APPENDIX 3.1: USING ASSESSMENT PROTOCOLS

A number of assessment protocols are now becoming available for use in this country although these have largely been developed in North America. In addition, there is increasing attention to and information on asking difficult questions in a sensitive and appropriate manner.

Reis (1999) and colleagues in Canada have developed a range of useful screening instruments that are quick and easy to apply and allow important knowledge to be gained about possible abuse. These instruments were designed as part of a six-element assessment and intervention programme. Further details of these may be obtained from the authors, but an overview is provided in Pritchard (1999). Some key instruments are the following:

- *Brief Abuse Screen for the Elderly* (BASE). This is a simple and easy to complete procedure. It is best undertaken by a range of different practitioners over time. It relates to the particular situation under scrutiny and is adaptable to local and cultural conditions. It does presuppose an element of training because it requires practitioners to make a 'guess' about possible abuse.
- *The Caregiver Abuser Scale* (CASE). Again, it is a quick and easy measure but it is completed by caregivers rather than practitioners. It is designed to be as non-threatening as possible and is applied to all caregivers irrespective of whether or not abuse is suspected. It is an information-gathering tool. The greater the number of 'yes' scores, the more likely it is that abuse is taking place. All 'yes' scores are investigated further and thus a proactive approach is taken.
- *Indicators of Abuse Checklist* (IOA). This checklist provides a summary of high-risk signals of abuse in a particular case. It helps to sensitise the practitioner to important signals of abuse, is a useful training tool and serves as an on-going reminder of the issues in a particular case. It does rely on the earlier assessments by and the opinions of the practitioner.
- *Abuse Intervention Description* (AID). This acts as an intervention planner and allows the monitoring of progress and intervention. This scale prioritises issues and concerns arising from other scales and then indicates what needs to be done.

Interventions in elder abuse

THEORETICAL FRAMEWORKS

A number of models have been developed to further the understanding of elder abuse, and these are important in determining the interventive approach to be taken. The particular understanding that practitioners or agencies bring to elder abuse will affect the way in which they intervene. If intervention strategies are founded on principles of empowerment, they will not only satisfy the demands of social work and health care values but are also more likely to be received and appreciated in that they acknowledge the strengths, potential, wants and wishes of the older person.

> *The goals for intervening in a case of senior mistreatment are to attempt to stop or reduce the risk of abuse. This is not a simple task. Any intervention plan must take into account the wishes of the victim.* (Lithwick, 1999, p. 366).

In *psychopathological models* the abuse is linked to the social and mental health status of the abuser. Whilst this model may only apply to a small number of cases, it does offer the possibility of positive and effective intervention. Violent behaviour patterns are seen as learned responses that can be unlearned and replaced by more adaptive behaviours. This model suggests that while protection and alternatives can be offered to the person who is being abused, the primary objective of the intervention is to change the actions of the abuser.

The *vulnerability hypothesis* may derive much of its influence and acceptance from the popular beliefs that people become vulnerable as a result of age. This view is often internalised by the older individuals themselves. In this model it is suggested that incapacities and impairments render a person frail, and therefore at risk of exploitation. If dependency causes vulnerability and stress in caregivers then intervention must seek to reduce dependency and increase the benefits of social exchanges with caregivers.

There are clear links between the vulnerability hypothesis and *situational models*. Whilst situational stress has been challenged as a causal explanation for abuse, a person's interactions with his or her environment and his or her perceptions of events and situations will affect future actions. Social workers and health care practitioners should work to increase positive interactions, reduce adverse ones and seek to influence individuals' perceptions of situations in a positive, stress-reducing way.

The importance of theoretical models for the practitioner lies not only in their explanatory and predictive power but also, and primarily, in planning an effective response. For instance if the abuse reflects learned behaviours and actions, a behavioural approach is indicated. The person under stress, on the other hand, will no doubt need practical help and support to reduce those demands and obligations that are perceived to be stress-inducing. Of course in practice it is unlikely that cases of elder abuse can be neatly compartmentalised and a combination of approaches is likely to work best and deal holistically with those involved.

INTERVENTIONS

The search for effective interventions is still in its early stages in the UK. There is a continuing debate between those who stress the need for increased protective services and those who advocate the development of therapeutic and support services. This echoes the wider debate on domestic violence. Some commentators highlight what they see as the lack of protective legislation, but also indicate the rich and flexible responses possible under the existing legislation.

It is probably at the level of legal intervention that the debate about the uniqueness or otherwise of elder abuse is most pressing. It may be argued that an approach that acknowledges uniqueness is preferable in order to avoid association with child abuse frameworks that may pathologise, marginalise and prevent the development of a response designed to educate society as a whole. Marking out elder abuse as unique would extend our understanding of the phenomenon from its location within the family in which it is associated with domestic violence. Unfortunately, in an ageist society the uniqueness approach may also confirm the stereotype of the elderly as dependent and vulnerable which might lead to marginalisation. It is possible to frame a response according to the dimensions, setting and type of abuse identified. This need not detract from identifying and acknowledging the significance of the abuse of older people and would allow the most effective interventions to be offered in each individual case. It would acknowledge the importance of the transfer of knowledge, skills and values across settings and client groups.

There are a number of options available to social and health care practitioners when working in the field of elder abuse. These are outlined according to three levels of intervention:

- Legal options.
- Social care responses.
- Psychological and psychotherapeutic approaches.

LEGAL OPTIONS

Social workers are perhaps treading familiar ground when working in the context of legislation. There are a number of legal options available at present, although these have not been consolidated. Legislation allows for civil actions in tort and criminal action. As a result of wide consultation and campaigns for stronger legal powers, the Law Commission (1995) suggested that legal reforms and the consolidation of existing legislation should be undertaken. The Commission's report attempted to balance the protection of vulnerable people at risk with people's right to exercise choice. A step-by-step approach was suggested.

- The power to enter.
- The power to apply for a warrant.
- The power to apply for an assessment order.
- The power to apply for a 'temporary protection order' enabling removal (Law Commission, 1995, paras 9.19–34).

The government did not frame legislation on the basis of this report but issued a further consultation paper. In fact there has been a move away from the earlier calls for greater protective legislation, and powers of entry remain limited for practitioners. Reflection on the North American experience of legislation without corresponding resource provision may have been influential here. In the light of evidence from the Alzheimer's Disease Society it was suggested that greater legal powers could in fact be abusive in themselves (Alzheimer's Disease Society, 1993; Penhale and Kingston, 1995).

The Mental Health Act, 1983 offers possibilities for protection but could lead to people being further abused by professional intervention. The Act allows a social worker or the person's nearest relative to make an application for admission to hospital (Sections 2 and 3) or for a guardianship order (Section 7) for those whose mental health problem is of such a degree or nature that they warrant assessment under the Act. The terms of the Act may be invoked to prevent a vulnerable mentally ill person from being further abused or to remove them from the danger of self-neglect and harm. It is an action to which the vulnerable person is subject, it is imposed on the individual as a protective measure. The Act also warrants the protection of an older person from abuse by another person with a mental health problem.

It may be that more recent legislation can be invoked to protect older people. The Protection from Harassment Act, 1997 outlaws conduct that amounts to harassment of another person (Section 1). Those found guilty of harassment, including causing fear of violence on at least two occasions (Section 4), may be subject to a fine, imprisonment or a restraining injunction (Sections 2 and 3). It is also possible for the subject of harassment to claim damages for financial loss incurred or anxiety suffered as a result of the harassment.

The Family Law Act, 1996 may provide legal measures as it applies more generally to domestic violence in Part IV. The Act specifies when a spouse or partner is entitled to occupy the home but relates this mainly to younger adults and matters of child care and protection. It may be that the Act can be invoked in some cases of elder abuse. It is more likely, however, that the Act will be invoked to apply for a non-molestation order (Section 42). Such an order can, in fact, be made by the court in any family proceedings case if it is considered necessary in the interests of the health, safety and well-being of the person concerned.

What is important is that social workers are well-versed in the existing legislation and work protectively by providing information and advice, and by taking recourse to the law when necessary. This may include helping older people to gain access to legal advice and assistance should they so choose.

SOCIAL CARE RESPONSES

The Social Services Inspectorate study on elder abuse (Social Services Inspectorate, 1992), identifies a practical service response bound by principles designed to keep as many people in their own homes as possible. This remains the more traditional and often preferred response of local authority social services departments, but it is not the only response.

Intervention undertaken from the perspective of social and health care values is important. An empowerment-based approach can operate with carers and older people. Support groups and sensitive and flexible services can assist caregivers, whilst advocacy, self-help and collective action can assist the older person. All approaches must, however, be transparent. The values underpinning an action will influence that action and its conceptualisation.

A coordinated and multidisciplinary approach based on comprehensive assessment, care planning, service delivery, monitoring and reviewing is important. Training and clear procedural guidelines are also of paramount importance in establishing the basis for effective action. Procedures, policies and guidelines, however, are not the whole story. Whilst they assist the coordination of effective practice, they may obstruct and to some extent rigidify assessment, service delivery and practical support. Where further intervention is required they can help to identify this but they should not prescribe matters of delivery and process.

As we have noted, the traditional response of social services departments to identified and suspected abuse has been to increase the provision of practical care and support services. Whilst increased care services and practical support can relieve caregiver stress, they seem to do little to reduce the risk of harm. Homer and Gilleard (1994) reject the stress hypothesis in favour of a 'perpetrator-pathology' model, which involves helping the perpetrator to change. These two approaches – perpetrator-pathology and practical service delivery – are not, of course, mutually exclusive.

It has been suggested that behavioural approaches may be more effective. McCreadie (1996) argues that services are important but depend on the type of abuse, the reasons for it and the decision-making capacities of those involved.

Information on intervention practices in North America indicates that practical services do need to be on offer. In fact each individual state in the United States is responsible for developing and delivering appropriate services within its boundaries. Adult protective services (APSs) have been developed as a result of the move towards mandatory reporting of elder abuse in most states. Social workers, trained in working with abused and vulnerable adults, staff these teams. At present there is no such requirement in the UK, although APS-style pilot teams are being developed and are providing a useful response from which policy makers can learn. An APS-type model is being piloted in Gloucestershire, UK.

An important addition to service provision has recently been developed in the UK. The energy and commitment of Yvonne Craig, a social worker, has been instrumental in replicating the North American model of elder mediation. She defines elder mediation as:

> *a voluntary process in which elderly persons are enabled to make their own decisions in interpersonal conflicts with the help of trained independent workers, generally senior volunteers, who are concerned for the rights, interests and needs of all participants* (Craig, 1997, p. 7).

This approach is enabling and empowering. It encourages communication and decision making among those at the heart of the conflict. In this sense it concurs with the value bases of social and health care professionals. There is a need for a rigorous evaluation of elder mediation and a corresponding need for caution. Not all situations are open to mediation and negotiated conflict resolution. However, where appropriate, self-advocacy and mediation are useful additions to methods of dealing with elder abuse.

PSYCHOLOGICAL AND PSYCHOTHERAPEUTIC RESPONSES

Pritchard (1998) advocates the use of psychodynamic counselling. She believes this will assist older people who have been abused or those who abuse to work through unresolved issues that arose earlier in life and so integrate and establish their identities. Unfortunately this does not seem to be as good an option as it first appears. Social and health care workers are not necessarily suitably trained in the skilled deployment of psychoanalytic and psychodynamic approaches, nor do they have the time or the backing of their agencies to commit themselves to such ongoing work. Also, the growing trend towards evidence-based practice suggests that psychodynamic approaches in general may not be effective and are not always open to empirical validation. It is probably safe to say that approaches based on psychodynamic theories should only be carried out by highly trained and skilled practitioners. Excellent psychotherapeutic work is being undertaken with older people suffering from past trauma, especially war trauma (Hunt *et al.*, 1997). This is something that practitioners in residential care homes, nursing homes and hospital settings need to be aware of, in order to plan and deliver services that meet the needs of those in there care. It is likely, of course, that an increasing number of older people will benefit from more person-centred approaches to counselling, although there still may be constraints in terms of time, resources and skilled personnel. This will require an awareness of when to refer individuals to an appropriate agency or practitioner.

Research in North America suggests that cognitive and behavioural approaches are useful in responding to situations of abuse. Work with people experiencing domestic violence is beginning to reveal the potential here. Anger-management training programmes for care staff in institutional settings echo this finding. Such intervention is found to:

- Reduce stress.
- Promote relaxation and self-control.
- Assist in the identification of triggers.
- Promote the adoption of more adaptable thinking and behaviours .

Research into crisis intervention and cognitive and behavioural strategies where violence and aggression are issues has revealed similar results. Family-based approaches, derived from structural and strategic family therapies, have also been proposed and adapted to the UK context. Whilst these offer exciting opportunities, the lack of development and resourcing in the UK has prevented the rigorous testing of such methods.

One of the most developed approaches is the staircase model (Breckman and Adelman, 1988). Intervention proceeds through three stages – reluctance, recognition and rebuilding – with competent victims of elder abuse. The limitations are, of course, that the model does not suggest intervention measures for the abuser, which may be more warranted, and incompetent victims are excluded. Despite this, the model lends itself to application across various settings.

At first, when dealing with *reluctance*, the practitioner assists the client to identify feelings of isolation, guilt and self-blame. The intention is to increase self-acceptance and to identify appropriate alternative thought patterns and behaviours. Practical support and information is provided at this stage. However an approach similar to rational-emotive-behavioural therapy is also suggested. Irrational and distorted thinking and imperative statements are identified and matched against reality. During the second stage, *recognition*, the individual is encouraged to seek more adaptive and rational thought patterns, to increase self-acceptance and to work to reduce his or her social isolation. In the final stage, *rebuilding*, the individual pursues a range of active strategies for living free from abuse and mistreatment, with the experience of self-efficacy, learning and knowledge of appropriate responses.

The form of intervention adopted is often indicative of the individual practitioner's or agency's theoretical and conceptual base. Thus an approach based on the service delivery perspective would suggest that the relief of caregiver stress is indicated, and the legal model implies a vulnerability/dependency conceptualisation. It may be inferred therefore, that the use of cognitive and behavioural approaches reflects a belief that elder abuse results from pathology, stress and situational factors, thus excluding wider socio-economic causes. Whilst these approaches certainly have clear theoretical implications they do not privilege one concept above another. Rather they acknowledge a multimodel approach to understanding. A great advantage of the approaches is that they acknowledge their limitations. They transcend barriers and present the options available in given situations under certain circumstances. The clarity of behaviours, interactions and interacting factors and situations allow for well-formulated and measurable actions for change. The approaches also take into account individual case factors and acknowledge the fundamental importance of participation in the process. Sadler (1994, p. 35) summarises this well.

> *in the rush to address this problem, we must not lose sight of the older people whom we are keen to help. Further research into what they want us to do is essential if we are to respond in a manner which does not disempower victims even further.*

The cognitive and behavioural approaches offer a return of control, the employment of effective coping strategies and a non-stigmatising and effective strategy for dealing with abuse: they are situation-specific. Perhaps their most effective use is with people who have abused, and especially where there is a degree of perceived stress.

> *Jim Franklin and his wife moved nearer their daughter and family following his retirement. Enid, his wife, enjoyed retirement to the full, engaging in a wide range of activities. This came to an abrupt end when Jim had a stroke, which left him very weak physically and necessitated* ▶

◄ *Enid spending considerable time caring for him.
Her frustration grew to the point where she began
to blame him personally for the situation. She
began to shout at him and on occasion hit him
across the face.
With the help of a social worker Enid learnt to
recognise the trigger points for her frustration and
anger, and this combined with relaxation
techniques, enabled Enid to regain control of the
situation. She also looked with the social worker at
practical and respite services that would assist her
and Jim. Furthermore, by identifying her feelings of
blame and guilt at the way she was acting, Enid
was able, with the social worker's support, to
challenge, dispute and replace these emotions with
a clear acknowledgement of her difficult situation.
This allowed her to take stock and plan her future.*
(author's case study)

Cognitive and behavioural techniques are at their most
useful when there is clear agreement among the parties
involved. One of the benefits of these approaches is the
behavioural, affective and cognitive changes that can
result. They also accord well with social work and health
care values, partnership, empowerment, change and hope.
Cognitive and behavioural approaches are transferable to
other settings and provide those involved with alternative
coping strategies.

INTEGRATED APPROACHES

There has been increasing interest in integrated and
multimodel approaches. These cover all aspects of elder
abuse but can relate to the particular role of an agency or
practitioner. The use of a range of interventive responses
reflects more appropriately the complexities of social work
and health care practice. Sadler (1994) examines responses
to elder abuse from an Australian perspective. He stresses
the importance of the social context, personal support, the
provision of practical and financial support and advocacy.
In his review of interventions and research at the Hornsby
Kuring-gai Geriatric and Rehabilitation Service he isolates
five key elements of effective intervention:

> - Multidimensional assessment.
> - Attention to the emotional needs of victims and abusers.
> - High levels of well-coordinated services.
> - A recognition that a long history of domestic violence is unlikely to be changed quickly.
> - Institutional care should depend upon the severity of the disability, not the type of abuse.

This is not dissimilar to a comprehensive assessment, care plan and intervention strategy that could be undertaken within the care management approach in the UK.

Phillipson and Biggs (1995) distil a variety of approaches according to the foci of intervention, including exhausted caregivers, physically and mentally impaired caregivers who are not dependent on family members for support, independent elders abused by non-caregiving family members and abuse in institutional settings. This multimodal approach is perhaps the best one for the complex area of elder abuse. Policies affect service delivery and agencies work to specific briefs and legislation. This emphasises the need to work together in ways that will improve individual practice and agency service delivery, and encourage the development of policies that are inclusive of older people and their rights.

In social and health care a mix of effective interventive approaches is necessary. The types of intervention offered will, to some extent, reflect each agency's policy and procedures and will be based on social policy and legislation. It is at the inter- and intrapersonal levels that social and health care workers may have more scope to develop care plans and methods for intervening effectively to reduce distress, increase choice, capacity and safety. It is important for practitioners to approach each case with a reflective and openmind, and to build a body of case knowledge and develop their understanding and approaches with reference to contemporary research and practice.

CONCLUSION

It is often the case that service users do not acknowledge their difficulties or the need for change. When risks are not acknowledged matters become much more difficult. Questions of ethics arise in implementing programmes without the participation or consent of others involved. It is, however, possible to work with people who do not agree they have a problem. There needs to be a balance between the right of individuals to choose their own lifestyles and deal with their own risks and the protective responsibilities that social and health care workers are charged with delivering.

Epilogue

Elder abuse happens. If social and health care practitioners do not recognise this before making a comprehensive assessment or intervening in a situation identified as abusive they may compound, collude with or condone abuse. Elder abuse is a serious issue for which local authority social services departments have been given a lead role.
The impact of elder abuse and the extent of the problem is being increasingly recognised by the government and helping organisations. The needs of those who have been abused and the necessity to work with those who have abused are also increasingly acknowledged. However the debates on the matter are complex and fraught with disagreement and confusion. This can be clearly seen in the various definitions of elder abuse and equally so in other aspects of elder abuse.

The legal and policy base for social work and health care remains fragmented, but there are still options available to practitioners. One of the greatest needs is for practitioners to adopt a consolidated approach to elder abuse from the level of policy making to the level of practice. It is incumbent on individual practitioners to ensure that their knowledge base is sufficient to practice at the level in question. There is also an obvious need for training and guidance to be provided by agencies working with elder abuse. Likewise a response is necessary from educational institutions to guarantee that tomorrow's practitioners are equipped with up-to-date knowledge on all aspects of the problem. This should include information on effective interventions as this becomes available.

Such measures will assist practitioners to undertake assessments, and to plan, implement and evaluate interventions aimed at improving the quality of life of older people who have experienced abuse. It will also help practitioners to reduce the risk of further abuse occurring. We must stress that the greatest overall need is for continued emphasis on respect for individuals, difference and diversity, and the promotion of choice, privacy and individual strengths. We must also stress the clear need for us all continually to challenge discrimination and disadvantage at the social, organisational and personal levels. Without this commitment, we are contributing to the maintenance of abuse and are unlikely to achieve any lasting resolution of the socially malign problem of elder abuse.

References

Action on Elder Abuse (1995) 'Action on Elder Abuse's definition of elder abuse' *Action on Elder Abuse Bulletin*, May/June

Aitken, L and Griffin, G (1996) *Gender Issues in Elder Abuse* London, Sage

Alzheimer's Disease Society (1993) *Position Paper on Prevention of Elder Abuse* London: Alzheimer's Disease Society

Barnett, O, Miller-Perrin, C and Perrin, R (1997) *Family Violence across the Lifespan: An Introduction* Thousand Oaks, Sage

Bennett, G, Kingston, P and Penhale, B (1997) *The Dimensions of Elder Abuse* Basingstoke, Macmillan

Breckman, R S and Adelman, R D (1988) *Strategies for Helping Victims of Elder Mistreatment* Newbury Park, CA, Sage

Browne, K and Herbert, M (1997) *Preventing Family Violence* Chichester, John Wiley and Sons

Craig, Y (1997) *Elder Abuse and Mediation: Exploratory studies in America, Britain and Europe*, Aldershot, Avebury

Curtis, Z (1993) 'On being a woman in the pensioners movement', in Johnson, J and Slater, R (eds) *Ageing and Later Life* London, Sage, pp193–9

Department of Health (2000) *No Secrets: Guidance on developing and implementing multi-agency policies and procedures to protect vulnerable adults from abuse* London, Department of Health

Department of Health/SSI (1996) *Domestic Violence and Social Care* London, HMSO

Grafstrom, M, Norberg, A and Wimblad, B (1992) 'Abuse is in the eye of the beholder: Reports by family members about abuse of demented persons in home care: A total population-based study' *Scandinavian Journal of Social Medicine* 21, pp 247–55

Hague, G and Malos, E (1998) 'Interagency approaches to domestic violence and the role of social services' *British Journal of Social Work* 28, (3) pp 369–86

Homer, A and Gilleard, C (1994) 'The effect of in-patient respite care on elderly patients and their carers' *Age and Ageing* 23, pp 274–6

Hunt, L Marshall, M and Rowlings, C (1997) *Past Trauma in Later Life* London, Jessica Kingsley Press

Jack, R (1994) 'Dependence, power and violation: gender issues in abuse of elderly people by formal carers' in Eastman, M (ed.) *Old Age Abuse* 2nd edition, London, Chapman-Hall, pp 77–92

Kaufman, M (1994) 'Men, feminism, and men's contradictory experiences of power' in Brod, H and Kaufman, M (eds) *Theorizing Masculinities* Thousand Oaks, CA, Sage, pp 142–63

Lachs, M S, Williams, C, O'Brien, S, Hurst, L and Horwitz, R (1997) 'Risk factors for reported elder abuse and neglect: A nine-year observational cohort study' *The Gerontologist* 37(4), pp 469–74

Law Commission (1995) *Mental Incapacity*, Law Commission report no 231, London, HMSO

Lithwick, M (1999) 'The dynamics of senior mistreatment and the options for intervention', in J Pritchard (ed.) *Elder Abuse Work: Best practice in Britain and Canada* London, Jessica Kingsley Press, pp 354–77

Lord Chancellor's Department (1999) *Making Decisions* Cmnd 4465, London, HMSO

Mandelstam, M (1999) *Community Care Practice and the Law* 2nd edition, London, Jessica Kingsley Press

McCreadie, C (1996) *Elder Abuse: update on research* London, Age Concern Institute of Gerontology

Middleton, L (1997) *The Art of Assessment* Birmingham, Venture Press

Mullender, A (1996) *Rethinking Domestic Violence: The social work and probation response* London, Routledge

National Center on Elder Abuse (1998) T*he National Elder Abuse Incidence Study* http://www.aoa.gov/abuse/report/default.html (Accessed Nov. 1998)

Nolan, M (1999) 'Enhancing the quality of care in residential and nursing homes: more than just a professional responsibility', in Glendenning, F and Kingston, P (eds) *Elder Abuse and Neglect in Residential Settings* New York, Haworth Press, pp 61–77

Ogg, J and Bennett, G C J (1992) 'Elder abuse in Britain' *British Medical Journal* 305, pp:998–9

Parker, J and Penhale, B (1998) *Forgotten People: Positive approaches to dementia care* Aldershot, Ashgate/Arena

Parsloe, P (ed.) (1999) *Risk Assessment in Social Care and Social Work* London, Jessica Kingsley Press

Penhale, B and Kingston, P (1995) 'Social perspectives on elder abuse' in Kingston, P and Penhale, B (eds) *Family Violence and the Caring Professions* Basingstoke, Macmillan, pp 222–44

Phillipson, C and Biggs, S (1995) 'Elder abuse: a critical overview', In P Kingston and B Penhale (eds) *Family Violence and the Caring Professions* Basingstoke, Macmillan, pp 181–203

Pritchard, J (1998) 'Psychodynamic counselling and older people who have been abused' in Bear, Z (ed) *Good Practice in Counselling People who Have Been Abused* London, Jessica Kingsley Press, pp 117–32

Pritchard, J (ed.) (1999) *Elder Abuse Work: Best practice in Britain and Canada* London, Jessica Kingsley Press

Reis, M (1999) 'Innovative interventions when seniors are abused', in Pritchard, J (ed.) *Elder Abuse Work: Best practice in Britain and Canada* London, Jessica Kingsley Press, pp 378–407

Sadler, P (1994) 'What helps? Elder abuse interventions and research' *Australian Social Work* 47 (4) pp 27–36

Social Services Inspectorate (SSI) (1991a) *Care Management and Assessment: the Practitioners' guide* London, HMSO

Social Services Inspectorate (SSI) (1991b) *Care Management and Assessment: the Managers' guide* London, HMSO

Social Services Inspectorate (SSI) (1992) *Confronting Elder Abuse* London, HMSO

Social Services Inspectorate (SSI) (1993) *No Longer Afraid: The safeguard of older people in domestic settings* London, HMSO

Social Services Inspectorate (SSI) (1995) *Abuse of older people in domestic settings: a report of two SSI seminars* London, HMSO

Stanley, N, Manthorpe, J and Penhale, B (1999) *Institutional Abuse Perspectives across the life course* London, Routledge

Stevenson, O (1999) *Elder Protection in Residential Care: what can we learn from Child Protection?* London, Department of Health

Stevenson, O and Parsloe, P (1993) *Community Care and Empowerment* York, Joseph Rowntree Foundation

Sutton, C (1994) *Social Work, Community Work and Psychology* Leicester, BPS Books

Thompson, N (1998) *Promoting Equality* Basingstoke, Macmillan

Whittaker, T (1995) 'Gender and elder abuse', in Arber, S and Ginn, J (eds) *Connecting Gender and Ageing: A sociological approach* Buckingham, Open University Press, pp 144–57

Whittaker, T (1996) 'Elder abuse', In Fawcett, B, Featherstone, B, Hearn, J and Toft, C (eds) *Violence and Gender Relations: Theories and Interventions* London, Sage, pp 147–60